Baby
Gorillas

Mary Elizabeth Salzmann

Consulting Editor, Diane Craig, M.A./Reading Specialist

Sandcastle

An Imprint of Abdo Publishing
www.abdopublishing.com

www.abdopublishing.com

Published by Abdo Publishing, a division of ABDO, PO Box 398166, Minneapolis, Minnesota 55439. Copyright © 2015 by Abdo Consulting Group, Inc. International copyrights reserved in all countries. No part of this book may be reproduced in any form without written permission from the publisher. SandCastle™ is a trademark and logo of Abdo Publishing.

Printed in the United States of America, North Mankato, Minnesota

102014
012015

Editor: Alex Kuskowski
Content Developer: Nancy Tuminelly
Cover and Interior Design and Production: Mighty Media, Inc.
Photo Credits: Shutterstock

Library of Congress Cataloging-in-Publication Data

Salzmann, Mary Elizabeth, 1968- author.
 Baby gorillas / Mary Elizabeth Salzmann.
    pages cm. -- (Baby animals)
 Audience: Ages 4-9.
 ISBN 978-1-62403-510-4
1. Gorilla--Infancy--Juvenile literature. I. Title.
 QL737.P94S25 2015
 599.8841392--dc23
                        2014023426

SandCastle™ Level: Beginning

SandCastle™ books are created by a team of professional educators, reading specialists, and content developers around five essential components—phonemic awareness, phonics, vocabulary, text comprehension, and fluency—to assist young readers as they develop reading skills and strategies and increase their general knowledge. All books are written, reviewed, and leveled for guided reading, early reading intervention, and Accelerated Reader® programs for use in shared, guided, and independent reading and writing activities to support a balanced approach to literacy instruction. The SandCastle™ series has four levels that correspond to early literacy development. The levels are provided to help teachers and parents select appropriate books for young readers.

EMERGING · **BEGINNING** · TRANSITIONAL · FLUENT

Contents

Baby Gorillas

Gorillas usually have one baby at a time.

Mother gorillas hold their babies.

Mother gorillas help their babies walk.

A baby gorilla can ride on its mother's back.

Baby gorillas get milk from their mothers. They also eat plants.

Baby gorillas play together.

Some baby gorillas live in zoos. They are good climbers.

Baby gorillas like to swing on ropes.

Baby gorillas stay with their mothers for about four years.

Did You Know?

▶ Gorillas are from **Africa**.

▶ There are two gorilla **species**. They are the eastern gorilla and the western gorilla.

▶ A group of gorillas is called a troop.

▶ Gorillas live about 40 years.

Gorilla Quiz

Read each sentence below. Then decide whether it is true or false.

1. Mother gorillas hold their babies.

2. Mother gorillas help their babies walk.

3. A baby gorilla can ride on its mother's back.

4. Baby gorillas don't like to swing on ropes.

5. Baby gorillas stay with their mothers for about four months.

Answers: 1. True 2. True 3. True 4. False 5. False

Glossary

Africa – the second-largest continent. Nigeria, Congo, and Zaire are in Africa.

species – a group of related living beings.